KAHLIL GIBRAN'S

Little Book of Life

KAHLIL GIBRAN'S

LITTLE BOOK OF LIFE

NEIL DOUGLAS-KLOTZ

AMARYLLIS

An imprint of Manjul Publishing House

AMARYLLIS

An imprint of Manjul Publishing House Pvt. Ltd.

• C-16, Sector 3, Noida, Uttar Pradesh 201 301, India

Website: www.manjulindia.com

Registered Office:

• 2nd Floor, Usha Preet Complex, 42 Malviya Nagar,
Bhopal 462 003 – India

Distribution Centres

Ahmedabad, Bengaluru, Chennai, Hyderabad,
Kochi, Kolkata, Mumbai, Noida, Pune

Published by arrangement with
Hampton Roads Publishing Company, Inc., USA.

ISBN 978-93-88241-07-6

Cover design by Manjul Publishing House Pvt. Ltd
Interior by Deborah Dutton

This edition first published in 2018
Fifth impression 2026

Printed and bound in India by Parksons Graphics Pvt. Ltd.

For all the immigrants who contribute to new cultures and civilizations

Contents

3. *Life's Human Journey* 69

4. *Seasons of Life* 103

5. *Paradoxical Life* 123

Introduction

For the past eighty years, the beautiful words of the Lebanese-American poet Kahlil Gibran have graced everything from greeting cards and wedding invitations to inspirational wall hangings and corporate motivational literature. By one account, Gibran is the third best-selling poet of all time, after Shakespeare and Lao-Tzu. Through short excerpts, largely extracted from his famous book *The Prophet*, most of us know him as a visionary voice of comfort, love, and tolerance.

As wonderful as this is, there is much more to Kahlil Gibran.

These new “little book” collections take a fresh look at Gibran’s words and wisdom taking into account the major influences on his life: his Middle Eastern culture, nature mysticism, and spirituality. One could easily argue that what the average reader of his time found exotic in Gibran is the way he clearly expressed a region that most regarded as a conundrum. A hundred years later, understanding this conundrum has moved beyond being an exotic pastime to becoming a matter of survival.

The book before you collects Gibran's words on "life." Future books in this series will collect Gibran's writings on love and relationships, on secrets of the spiritual path, and on wisdom for everyday life.

To English speakers, the word *life* remains abstract. Do we mean the life-span of a human being, the course of daily life, or the philosophical premise of existence? Who or what has life?

To a Middle Easterner, the word *life* has a very specific meaning. Whether in biblical Hebrew, the Aramaic of Jesus, or the literary Arabic in which Gibran wrote many of his early works, life means life energy and vitality. What is important is the way someone or something expresses this life, not the way he, she, or it appears. Life (*hayy* in Arabic) is related to the common word for breath in the Semitic languages—a breath of life that is found in all of nature and throughout the universe.

The "unnameable Name" of God in the ancient Hebrew tradition is related to this word as is one of the "99 Beautiful Names" of God in the Islamic tradition. Whether earthly or heavenly life, temporal or eternal life, inner or outer life—to a Middle Eastern poet and mystic like Gibran it is all one life energy saturating everything we can see and feel, as well as what we can only imagine.

Because Gibran deliberately connects categories that most of us see as opposites, some critics have accused him of exploiting the simple literary device of paradox to artificially confuse and bemuse his readers. But seeing light and dark, inner and outer, good and evil as complements, not opposites, lies at the heart of Middle Eastern culture and philosophy. If there is only one life behind and within everything, then connections lie around every corner, so to speak.

According to one of his biographers, Suheil Bushrui, Gibran was heavily influenced by the mysticism of the 12th-century Andalusian Sufi Moinuddin Ibn Arabi. In Ibn Arabi's idea of the "unity of Being," the divine reality suffuses all of existence, yet is greater than anything we can experience or discover. Even more, Ibn Arabi implies that what we call life is a kind of experiment-in-process by which the Greater Reality (related to what Gibran calls the "Greater Soul") progressively learns more about itself through the life journeys of every plant, animal, human being, star, and galaxy, as well as an unnameable number of unseen beings.

Another major influence: Gibran was raised as a Maronite Christian, an Eastern church allied to the Roman Catholic, but which until the 18th century spoke and used in liturgy the Syriac language, related to Jesus' native Aramaic. According to Dr. Walid Phares, the Secretary General of the World Maronite Union, "the historic identity of the Maronite people is Aramaic, Syriac, and Eastern. . . . Maronites, particularly the national community that lived in Mount Lebanon and its peripheries for thirteen centuries, have maintained their historical identity despite attempts by regional powers, including Arab and Ottoman empires, to impose an alien identity."

This upbringing had two major effects on Gibran.

First, the Aramaic-speaking churches historically viewed Jesus, the prophet of Nazareth, as a human being, a small-s "son" of God, who uniquely fulfills his destiny and expresses the divine life in a way open to us all. In this sense, we can all become "children" of God, that is, of "Sacred Unity" (the literal translation of the Aramaic word for God, *Alaha*). Gibran's book *Jesus The Son of Man* takes the same viewpoint. In a very modern way, it tells the prophet's story from the viewpoints of many different people who knew him, some mentioned in the Bible, others not (like an old shepherd, an astrologer, and a neighbor and friend of Mary). Hearing their multiple (and sometimes conflicting) stories shows us that, for Gibran, Jesus was not a figure that could be encapsulated in any one creed or contained within the walls of any one church.

As Gibran writes in one of the selections contained in this book:

Once every hundred years Jesus of Nazareth
meets Jesus of the Christian
in a garden among the hills of Lebanon.

And they talk long.
And each time Jesus of Nazareth goes away
saying to Jesus of the Christian,
"My friend, I fear we shall never, never agree."

Second, as Dr. Phares writes above, the Maronites, and Gibran in particular, were strong believers in the self-determination of the Syrian people. The word *Syrian* here was used in a cultural sense, since the boundaries of the state of Syria were not set until after the First World War. Gibran worked for various "Syrian" causes before the end of war, which he saw as an opportunity for his people to free themselves from a corrupt Ottoman empire. Like many of his contemporaries, he felt betrayed by the Sykes-Picott Agreement in which the victorious Western powers essentially divided the post-Ottoman Middle East into nation states for their own influence and convenience. We are still living with the consequences of this a hundred years later.

Gibran's deep love for his native country, his belief in the essential goodness of its people, his connection to its land and nature shine through many of these selections. In one originally entitled "To Young Americans of Syrian Origin," published in 1926, Gibran writes:

"I believe that you can say to Emerson and Whitman and James, 'In my veins runs the blood of the poets and wise men of old, and it is my desire to come to you and receive, but I shall not come with empty hands.'"

On the actual editing: it is clear that Gibran was helped with his grammar and punctuation by various people, particularly his longtime muse Mary Haskell. As the way we read has changed over the past hundred years, so has grammar, so I have re-punctuated or re-lined many selections in order to bring out the rhythm of Gibran's voice for the modern reader.

As far as Gibran's use of gender-inclusive or -exclusive terms goes, I have mostly taken a hands-off approach. Gibran often refers to God as "he," but he also refers to Life as "she" and makes frequent references to "goddesses." The one exception to this policy is that I have substituted "humanity" for "mankind." It does not disturb the rhythm of Gibran's voice, is more faithful to the underlying (and gender neutral) Arabic word he was thinking of, and is a more accurate way of including us all.

In selecting the material for this book, I have placed well-known sayings of Gibran next to lesser known ones, organized by the various views of "life" that he expressed. Some of Gibran's sayings are comforting and easy to understand, some puzzling, some disturbing. Like many Middle Eastern mystics, he seems to have felt that periods of being puzzled or disturbed were as important as those of comfort to help bring balance and healing to his own somewhat chaotic personal life, as well as to the lives of his readers. Perhaps this willingness to embrace all of life has something to do with his enduring appeal for us.

—Neil Douglas-Klotz
Fife, Scotland
June 2017

1

Listening to Nature's Life

Taking time to listen to the natural world reveals a new dimension of being human. It is as if all of nature were already within us, reminding us of our connection to the one life we share.

The Law of Nature

Before the throne of freedom, the trees rejoice with the frolicsome breeze and enjoy the rays of the sun and the beams of the moon.

Through the ears of freedom the birds whisper, and around freedom they flutter to the music of the brooks.

Throughout the sky of freedom the flowers breathe their fragrance, and before freedom's eyes they smile when day comes.

Everything lives on earth according to the law of nature, and from that law emerges the glory and joy of liberty.

Yet humanity denied itself this fortune, because it set for the God-given soul a limited and earthly law of its own.

It made for itself strict rules and built a narrow and painful prison in which it secluded humanity's affections and desires. It dug out a deep grave in which it buried humanity's heart and purpose.

If individuals, through the dictates of their souls, declare their withdrawal from society and violate the law, their fellows will say they are rebels worthy of exile or infamous creatures worthy only of execution.

Will people remain slaves of self-confinement until the end of the world?

Or will they be freed by the passing of time and live in the spirit and for the spirit?

Will they insist upon staring downward and backward at the earth?

Or will they turn their eyes toward the sun so they will not see the shadow of their bodies amongst the skulls and thorns?

Said a Blade of Grass

Said a blade of grass to an autumn leaf:

"You make such a noise falling! You scatter all my winter dreams."

Said the leaf indignant:

"Lowborn and low-dwelling! Song-less, peevish thing! You live not in the upper air and you cannot tell the sound of singing."

Then the autumn leaf lay down upon the earth and slept.

And when spring came she waked again—and she was a blade of grass.

And when it was autumn and her winter sleep was upon her, and above her through all the air the leaves were falling, she muttered to herself:

"O, these autumn leaves! They make such noise! They scatter all my winter dreams."

Three Dogs

Three dogs were basking in the sun and conversing.

The first dog said dreamily, "It is indeed wondrous to be living in this day of dogdom. Consider the ease with which we travel under the sea, upon the earth, and even in the sky. And meditate for a moment upon the inventions brought forth for the comfort of dogs, even for our eyes and ears and noses."

And the second dog spoke and he said, "We are more heedful of the arts. We bark at the moon more rhythmically than did our forefathers. And when we gaze at ourselves in the water, we see that our features are clearer than the features of yesterday."

Then the third dog spoke and said, "But what interests me most and beguiles my mind is the tranquil understanding existing between dogdoms."

At that very moment they looked, and lo, the dogcatcher was approaching.

The three dogs sprang up and scampered down the street.

And as they ran the third dog said, "For God's sake, run for your lives! Civilization is after us!"

Shadows

A fox looked at his shadow at sunrise and said,

"I will have a camel for lunch today."

And all morning he went about looking for camels.

But at noon he saw his shadow again—and he said,

"A mouse will do."

Song of the Rain

I am dotted silver threads,
dropped from heaven by the gods.
Nature then takes me to adorn her fields and
valleys.

I am beautiful pearls,
plucked from the crown of Ishtar
by the daughter of dawn to embellish the
gardens.

When I cry, the hills laugh.
When I humble myself, the flowers rejoice.
When I bow, all things are elated.

The field and the cloud are lovers,
and between them I am a messenger of mercy.
I quench the thirst of one,
I cure the ailment of the other.

The voice of thunder declares my arrival.
The rainbow announces my departure.
I am like earthly life,
which begins at the feet of the mad elements
and ends under the upraised wings of death.

I emerge from the heart of the sea
and soar with the breeze.
When I see a field in need,
I descend and embrace
the flowers and the trees
in a million little ways.

I touch gently at the windows
with my soft fingers,
and my announcement is a welcome song.
All can hear,
but only the sensitive can understand.

The heat in the air gives birth to me,
but in turn I kill it,
as woman overcomes man
with the strength she takes from him.

I am the sigh of the sea,
the laughter of the field,
the tears of heaven.

So with love—
sighs from the deep sea of affection,
laughter from the colorful field of the spirit,
tears from the endless heaven of memories.

A Hyena and a Crocodile

Upon the bank of the Nile at eventide, a hyena met a crocodile, and they stopped and greeted one another.

The hyena spoke and said, "How goes the day with you, sir?"

And the crocodile answered, saying, "It goes badly with me. Sometimes in my pain and sorrow I weep, and then the creatures always say, 'They are but crocodile tears.' And this wounds me beyond all telling."

Then the hyena said, "You speak of your pain and your sorrow, but think of me also, for a moment. I gaze at the beauty of the world, its wonders and its miracles, and out of sheer joy I laugh even as the day laughs. And then the people of the jungle say, 'It is but the laughter of a hyena.'"

TWO OYSTERS

Said one oyster to a neighboring oyster,

"I have a very great pain within me. It is heavy and round and I am in distress."

And the other oyster replied with haughty complacence,

"Praise be to the heavens and to the sea, I have no pain within me. I am well and whole, both within and without."

At that moment a crab was passing by and heard the two oysters. And he said to the one who was well and whole, both within and without,

"Yes, you are well and whole, but the pain that your neighbor bears is a pearl of exceeding beauty."

Trees Are Poems

Trees are poems
that the earth writes upon the sky.
We fell them down and
turn them into paper
that we may record our emptiness.

THE RED EARTH

Said a tree to a man,

"My roots are in the deep red earth, and I shall give you of my fruit."

And the man said to the tree,

"How alike we are. My roots are also deep in the red earth. And the red earth gives you power to bestow upon me of your fruit, and the red earth teaches me to receive from you with thanksgiving."

THE FULL MOON

The full moon rose in glory upon the town, and all the dogs of that town began to bark at the moon.

Only one dog did not bark, and it said to the rest in a grave voice, "Awake not stillness from her sleep, nor bring you the moon to the earth with your barking."

Then all the dogs ceased barking, in awful silence.

But the dog who had spoken to them continued barking for silence the rest of the night.

The Supreme Ant

Three ants met on the nose of a man who was asleep in the sun. And after they had saluted one another, each according to the custom of its tribe, they stood there conversing.

The first ant said, "These hills and plains are the most barren I have known. I have searched all day for a grain of some sort, and there is none to be found."

Said the second ant, "I too have found nothing, though I have visited every nook and glade. This is, I believe, what my people call the soft, moving land where nothing grows."

Then the third ant raised its head and said, "My friends, we are standing now on the nose of the Supreme Ant, the mighty and infinite Ant, whose body is so great that we cannot see it, whose shadow is so vast that we cannot trace it, whose voice is so loud that we cannot hear it; and He is omnipresent."

When the third ant spoke thus the other ants looked at each other and laughed.

At that moment the man moved, and in his sleep raised his hand and scratched his nose, and the three ants were crushed.

The Pomegranate

Once when I was living in the heart of a pomegranate, I heard a seed saying, "Someday I shall become a tree, and the wind will sing in my branches, and the sun will dance on my leaves, and I shall be strong and beautiful through all the seasons."

Then another seed spoke and said, "When I was as young as you, I too held such views, but now that I can weigh and measure things, I see that my hopes were vain."

And a third seed spoke also, "I see in us nothing that promises so great a future."

And a fourth said, "But what a mockery our life would be without a greater future!"

Said a fifth, "Why dispute what we shall be, when we know not even what we are?"

But a sixth replied, "Whatever we are, that we shall continue to be."

And a seventh said, "I have such a clear idea how everything will be, but I cannot put it into words."

Then an eight spoke—and a ninth—and a tenth—and then many—until all were speaking, and I could distinguish nothing for the many voices.

And so I moved that very day into the heart of a quince, where the seeds are few and almost silent.

Solitude

Solitude is a silent storm
that breaks down all our dead branches.
Yet it sends our living roots deeper
into the living heart of the living earth.

Living Water

And in this lies my honor and my reward:
that whenever I come to the fountain to drink
I find the living water itself thirsty.
And it drinks me
while I drink it.

Other Seas

A fish said to another fish, "Above this sea of ours there is another sea, with creatures swimming in it—and they live there even as we live here."

The other fish replied, "Pure fancy! Pure fancy! When you know that everything that leaves our sea by even an inch, and stays out of it, dies. What proof have you of other lives in other seas?"

The River

In the valley of Kadisha[1] where the mighty river flows, two little streams met and spoke to one another.

One stream said, "How came you, my friend, and how was your path?"

And the other answered, "My path was most encumbered. The wheel of the mill was broken, and the master farmer who used to conduct me from my channel to his plants is dead. I struggled down, oozing with the filth of laziness in the sun. But how was your path, my brother?"

And the other stream answered and said, "Mine was a different path. I came down the hills among fragrant flowers and shy willows. Men and women drank of me with silvery cups, and little children paddled their rosy feet at my edges, and there was laughter all about me, and

1. A valley southeast of Tripoli in northern Lebanon. "Kadisha" or *Qadisha* means "holy" in Aramaic. The Kadisha valley's many natural caves were occupied since Paleolithic times and served as places of refuge for Christian and Muslim mystics. In 1998, UNESCO added the valley to its list of World Heritage Sites.

there were sweet songs. What a pity that your path was not so happy."

At that moment the river spoke with a loud voice and said, "Come in, come in, we are going to the sea! Come in, come in, speak no more. Be with me now. We are going to the sea. Come in, come in, for in me you shall forget your wanderings, sad or gay. Come in, come in! And you and I will forget all our ways when we reach the heart of our mother the sea."

CONTENTMENT AND THRIFT

Should nature heed
what we say of contentment
no river would seek the sea,
and no winter would turn to spring.
Should she heed all we say of thrift,
how many of us would be
breathing this air?

THE LOTUS-HEART

A lover and beloved at the time of Jesus:

Upon a day, my beloved and I were rowing upon the lake of sweet waters. And the hills of Lebanon were about us.

We moved beside the weeping willows, and the reflections of the willows were deep around us.

And while I steered the boat with an oar, my beloved took her lute and sang thus:

What flower save the lotus
knows the waters and the sun?
What heart save the lotus-heart
shall know both earth and sky?

Behold my love, the golden flower
that floats 'twixt deep and high
even as you and I float betwixt a love
that has forever been
and shall forever be.

Dip your oar, my love,
and let me touch my strings.
Let us follow the willows,
and let us leave not the water-lilies.

In Nazareth there lives a poet,
and his heart is like the lotus.
He has visited the soul of woman.
He knows her thirst is
growing out of the waters,
and her hunger is for the sun,
though all her lips are fed.

They say he walks in Galilee.
I say he is rowing with us.
Can you not see his face, my love?
Can you not see where the willow bough
and its reflection meet—
how he is moving as we move?

Beloved, it is good to know the youth of life.
It is good to know its singing joy.

Would that you might always have the oar
and I my stringed lute,
where the lotus laughs in the sun,
and the willow is dipping to the waters,
and his voice is upon my strings.

Dip your oar, my beloved,
and let me touch my strings.
There is a poet in Nazareth
who knows and loves us both.
Dip your oar, my lover,
and let me touch my strings.

The Shadow

Upon a June day the grass said to the shadow of an elm tree,

"You move to right and left over often, and you disturb my peace."

And the shadow answered and said,

"Not I, not I. Look skyward. There is a tree that moves in the wind to the east and to the west, between the sun and the earth."

And the grass looked up, and for the first time beheld the tree. And it said in its heart,

"Why, behold, there is a larger grass than myself!"

And the grass was silent.

The Serpent and the Lark

Said the serpent to the lark, "Thou flyest, yet thou canst not visit the recesses of the earth where the sap of life moveth in perfect silence."

And the lark answered, "Aye, thou knowest over much. Nay, thou art wiser than all things wise—pity thou canst not fly."

And as if he did not hear, the serpent said, "Thou canst not see the secrets of the deep, nor move among the treasures of the hidden empire. It was but yesterday I lay in a cave of rubies. It is like the heart of a ripe pomegranate, and the faintest ray of light turns into a flamerose. Who but me can behold such marvels?"

And the lark said, "None, none but thee can lie among the crystal memories of the cycles—pity thou canst not sing."

And the serpent said, "I know a plant whose root descends to the bowels of the earth, and the one who eats of that root becomes fairer than Astarte."

And the lark said, "No one, no one but thee could unveil the magic thought of the earth—pity thou canst not fly."

And the serpent said, "There is a purple stream that runneth under a mountain, and the one who drinketh of it shall become immortal even as the gods. Surely no bird or beast can discover that purple stream."

And the lark answered, "If thou willest, thou canst become deathless even as the gods—pity thou canst not sing."

And the serpent said, "I know a buried temple, which I visit once a moon. It was built by a forgotten race of giants, and upon its walls are graven the secrets of time and space, and the one who reads them shall understand that which passeth all understanding."

And the lark said, "Verily, if thou so desirest thou canst encircle with thy pliant body all knowledge of time and space—pity thou canst not fly."

Then the serpent was disgusted, and as he turned and entered into his hole he muttered, "Emptyheaded songster!"

And the lark flew away singing, "Pity thou canst not sing. Pity, pity, my wise one, thou canst not fly."

Frogs: On the Nature of Disturbance

Upon a summer day, a frog said to its mate, "I fear those people living in that house on the shore are disturbed by our night songs."

And its mate answered and said, "Well, do they not annoy our silence during the day with their talking?"

The frog said, "Let us not forget that we may sing too much in the night."

And its mate answered, "Let us not forget that they chatter and shout overmuch during the day."

Said the frog, "How about the bullfrog who disturbs the whole neighborhood with its God-forbidden booming?"

And its mate replied, "Aye, and what say you of the politician and the priest and the scientist who come to these shores and fill the air with noisy and rhymeless sound?"

Then the frog said, "Well, let us be better than these human beings. Let us be quiet at night, and keep our songs in our hearts, even though the moon calls for our rhythm and the stars for our rhyme. At least, let us be silent for a night or two, or even for three nights."

And its mate said, "Very well, I agree. We shall see what your bountiful heart will bring forth."

That night the frogs were silent, and they were silent the following night also, and again upon the third night.

And strange to relate, the talkative woman who lived in the house beside the lake came down to breakfast on that third day and shouted to her husband, "I have not slept these three nights. I was secure with sleep when the noise of the frogs was in my ear. But something must have happened. They have not sung now for three nights, and I am almost maddened with sleeplessness."

The frog heard this and turned to its mate and said, winking its eye, "And we were almost maddened with our silence, were we not?"

And its mate answered, "Yes, the silence of the night was heavy upon us. And I can see now that there is no need for us to cease our singing for the comfort of those who must needs fill their emptiness with noise."

And that night the moon called not in vain for their rhythm nor the stars for their rhyme.

Song of the Flower

I am a kind word uttered and repeated
by the voice of Nature.

I am a star fallen from the
blue tent upon the green carpet.

I am the daughter of the elements
with whom winter conceived,
to whom spring gave birth.
I was reared in the lap of summer,
and I slept in the bed of autumn.

At dawn I unite with the breeze
to announce the coming of light.
At eventide I join the birds
in bidding the light farewell.

The plains are decorated
with my beautiful colors,
and the air is scented with my fragrance.

As I embrace slumber
the eyes of night watch over me,
and as I awaken I stare at the sun,
which is the only eye of the day.

I drink dew for wine
and harken to the voices of the birds
and dance to the
rhythmic swaying of the grass.

I am the lover's gift.
I am the wedding wreath.
I am the memory of a moment of happiness.
I am the last gift of the living to the dead.
I am a part of joy and a part of sorrow.

But I look up high to see only the light
and never look down to see my shadow.

This is wisdom that humanity must learn.

SPRING IN LEBANON

Spring is beautiful everywhere, but it is most beautiful in Lebanon. It is a spirit that roams round the earth but hovers over Lebanon, conversing with kings and prophets, singing with the rivers the songs of Solomon and repeating with the Holy Cedars of Lebanon the memory of ancient glory.

Beirut, free from the mud of winter and the dust of summer, is like a bride in the spring, or like a mermaid sitting by the side of a brook drying her smooth skin in the rays of the sun.

Poets of the West think of Lebanon as a legendary place, forgotten since the passing of David and Solomon and the prophets, as the Garden of Eden became lost after the fall of Adam and Eve.

To those Western poets, the word Lebanon is a poetical expression associated with a mountain whose sides are drenched with the incense of the Holy Cedars. It reminds them of the temples of copper and marble standing stern and impregnable and of a herd of deer feeding in the valleys.

That night I saw Lebanon dreamlike with the eyes of a poet.

Thus the appearance of things changes according to the emotions.

We see magic and beauty in them, while the magic and beauty are really in ourselves.

2

Beauty and the Song of Life

Our life force increases as we bring more beauty into our lives, in whatever form we appreciate it. Life then moves us from within to create beauty and share it with others.

LIFE'S PURPOSE

We live only to discover beauty.
All else is a form of waiting.

Singing

If you sing of beauty
though alone in the heart of the desert
you will have an audience.

A great singer is he who sings our silences.

They say the nightingale
pierces his bosom with a thorn
when it sings its love song.
So do we all.
How else should we sing?

Genius is but a robin's song
at the beginning of a slow spring.

A madman is not less a musician
than you or myself,
only the instrument on which he plays
is a little out of tune.

When you sing,
the hungry hear you
with their stomachs.

Secrets of the Beauty of Life

The voice of Khalil the Heretic:

Vain are the beliefs and teachings that make humanity miserable, and false is the goodness that leads it into sorrow and despair. For it is humanity's purpose to be happy on this earth and lead the way to felicity and preach its gospel wherever it goes.

Those who do not see the kingdom of heaven in this life will never see it in the coming life.

We came not into this life by exile, but we came as innocent creatures of God, to learn how to worship the holy and eternal spirit and seek the hidden secrets within ourselves from the beauty of life.

This is the truth that I have learned from the teachings of the Nazarene.

This is the light that came from within me and showed me the dark corners of the convent that threatened my life.

This is the deep secret that the beautiful valleys and fields revealed to me when I was hungry, sitting lonely and weeping under the shadow of the trees.

This is the religion as the convent should impart it, as God wished it, as Jesus taught it.

The Poet

He is a link between this
and the coming world.
He is a pure spring from which
all thirsty souls may drink.

He is a tree watered by the river of beauty,
bearing fruit that the hungry heart craves.

He is a nightingale
soothing the depressed spirit
with his beautiful melodies.

He is a white cloud
appearing over the horizon,
ascending and growing
until it fills the face of the sky.
Then it falls on the flowers
in the field of Life,
opening their petals to admit the light.

He is an angel,
sent by the goddess
to preach the deity's gospel.

He is a brilliant lamp,
unconquered by darkness
and inextinguishable by the wind.
It is filled with oil by Ishtar of Love,
and lighted by Apollon of Music.

He is a solitary figure,
robed in simplicity and kindness.
He sits upon the lap of Nature
to draw his inspiration
and stays up in the silence of the night,
awaiting the descending of the spirit.

He is a sower who sows
the seeds of his heart
in the prairies of affection,
and humanity reaps the harvest
for her nourishment.

This is the poet,
whom the people ignore in this life,
and who is recognized only when
he bids the earthly world farewell
and returns to his arbor in heaven.

This is the poet,
who asks naught of humanity
but a smile.
This is the poet,
whose spirit ascends
and fills the firmament
with beautiful sayings,
yet the people deny themselves
his radiance.

Until when shall the people remain asleep?
Until when shall they continue to glorify those
who attain greatness by moments of advantage?
How long shall they ignore those
who enable them to see the beauty of their
    spirit,
symbol of peace and love?

Until when shall human beings
honor the dead and forget the living
who spend their lives encircled in misery
and who consume themselves
like burning candles to illuminate the way
for the ignorant and lead them
into the path of light?

Poet, you are the life of this life,
and you have triumphed over the ages
despite their severity.

Poet, you will one day rule the hearts,
and therefore your kingdom has no ending.

Poet, examine your crown of thorns.
You will find concealed in it
a budding wreath of laurel.

Art and Life

Four poets were sitting around a bowl of punch that stood on a table.

Said the first poet, "Methinks I see with my third eye the fragrance of this wine hovering in space like a cloud of birds in an enchanted forest."

The second poet raised his head and said, "With my inner ear I can hear those mistbirds singing. And the melody holds my heart, as the white rose imprisons the bee within her petals."

The third poet closed his eyes and stretched his arm upwards, and said, "I touch them with my hand. I feel their wings, like the breath of a sleeping fairy, brushing against my fingers."

Then the fourth poet rose and lifted up the bowl, and he said, "Alas, friends! I am too dull of sight and of hearing and of touch. I cannot see the fragrance of this wine, nor hear its song, nor feel the beating of its wings. I perceive but the wine itself. Now therefore must I drink it, that it may sharpen my senses and raise me to your blissful heights."

And putting the bowl to his lips, he drank the punch to the very last drop.

The three poets, with their mouths open, looked at him aghast, and there was a thirsty yet un-lyrical hatred in their eyes.

Pleasure Is a Freedom Song

Pleasure is a freedom song,
but it is not freedom.
It is the blossoming of your desires,
but it is not their fruit.
It is a depth calling unto a height,
but it is not the deep nor the high.

It is the caged taking wing,
but it is not space encompassed.

Aye, in very truth,
pleasure is a freedom song.
And I fain would have you sing it
with fullness of heart.

Yet I would not have you
lose your hearts
in the singing.

SINGING

Go you upon your way with singing,
but let each song be brief,
for only the songs that die young upon your lips
shall live in human hearts.

Tell a lovely truth in little words,
but never an ugly truth in any words.
Tell the maiden whose hair shines in the sun
that she is the daughter of the morning.
But if you shall behold the sightless,
say not to him that he is one with night.

Before the Throne of Beauty

One heavy day I ran away from the grim face of society and the dizzying clamor of the city and directed my weary step to the spacious alley. I pursued the beckoning course of the rivulet and the musical sounds of the birds until I reached a lonely spot where the flowing branches of the trees prevented the sun from touching the earth.

I stood there, and it was entertaining to my soul—my thirsty soul who had seen naught but the mirage of life instead of its sweetness.

I was engrossed deeply in thought, and my spirits were sailing the firmament when a houri, wearing a sprig of grapevine that covered part of her naked body and a wreath of poppies about her golden hair, suddenly appeared to me.

As she realized my astonishment, she greeted me saying, "Fear me not. I am the Nymph of the Jungle."

"How can beauty like yours be committed to live in this place? Please tell me who you are, and whence you come?" I asked.

She sat gracefully on the green grass and responded, "I am the symbol of Nature! I am the ever-virgin your forefathers worshipped, and to my honor they erected shrines and temples at Baalbek and Jubayl."

And I dared say, "But those temples and shrines were laid waste and the bones of my adoring ancestors became a part of the earth. Nothing was left to commemorate their goddess save a pitiful few and forgotten pages in the book of history."

She replied, "Some goddesses live in the lives of their worshippers and die in their deaths, while some live an eternal and infinite life. My life is sustained by the world of Beauty that you will see wherever you rest your eyes, and this Beauty is Nature itself. It is the beginning of the shepherd's joy among the hills, and a villager's happiness in the fields, and the pleasure of the awe-filled tribes between the mountains and the plains. This Beauty promotes the wise into the throne of Truth."

Then I said, "Beauty is a terrible power!"

And she retorted, "Human beings fear all things, even yourselves. You fear heaven, the source of spiritual peace. You fear Nature, the haven of rest and tranquility. You fear the God of goodness and accuse him of anger, while he is full of love and mercy."

After a deep silence, mingled with sweet dreams, I asked, "Speak to me of that beauty that the people interpret and define, each according to their own conception. I have seen her honored and worshipped in different ways and manners."

She answered, "Beauty is that which attracts your soul, and that which loves to give and not to receive. When you meet Beauty, you feel that the hands deep within your inner self are stretched forth to bring her into the domain of your heart. It is a magnificence combined of sorrow and joy. It is the unseen that you see, and the vague that you understand, and the mute that you hear—it is the Holy of Holies that begins in yourself and ends vastly beyond your earthly imagination."

Then the Nymph of the Jungle approached me and laid her scented hands upon my eyes. And as she withdrew, I found myself alone in the valley. When I returned to the city, whose turbulence no longer vexed me, I repeated her words:

"Beauty is that which attracts your soul, and that which loves to give and not to receive."

The Flute

Give me the ney[2] and sing
the secret song of being,
a song whose echo lasts even
till existence vanishes.

Have you, like me,
chosen the wilderness,
a house without limitations?
Have you followed the stream
and climbed the rocks,
bathing yourself in their fragrance,
drying yourself in their light?
Have you drunk the dawn
from goblets full of divine air?

Have you, like me,
sat down at dusk,

---

2. A Persian flute made of a hollow piece of reed or bamboo, made famous in Middle Eastern poetry by a reference in the opening lines of the *Mathnawi,* a poetic epic of the 12th-century Sufi Jelaluddin Rumi. There Rumi compares the reed plucked from the reedbed to make a flute to the soul cut off from and longing for Reality that is its home.

amid the glowing languor
of vines laden with grapes?
Have you lain down on the grass at night
and used the sky as your coverlet,
opening your heart to the future,
forgetful of the past?

Give me the ney and sing,
a song in tune with hearts.
The sounds of the ney will linger
beyond ailments and remedies.

Give me the ney and sing,
for human beings
are no more than
sketches traced in water.

Beauty

And a poet said, "Speak to us of beauty."

And Al Mustafa answered:

Where shall you seek beauty and how shall you find her unless she herself be your way and your guide?

And how shall you speak of her except she be the weaver of your speech?

The aggrieved and the injured say, "Beauty is kind and gentle. Like a young mother half-shy of her own glory she walks among us."

And the passionate say, "Nay, beauty is a thing of might and dread. Like the tempest she shakes the earth beneath us and the sky above us."

The tired and the weary say, "Beauty is of soft whisperings. She speaks in our spirit. Her voice yields to our silences like a faint light that quivers in fear of the shadow."

But the restless say, "We have heard her shouting among the mountains. And with her cries came the sound of hoofs and the beating of wings and the roaring of lions."

At night the watchers of the city say, "Beauty shall rise with the dawn from the east."

And at noontide the toilers and the wayfarers say, "We have seen her leaning over the earth from the windows of the sunset."

In winter say the snowbound, "She shall come with the spring, leaping upon the hills."

And in the summer heat the reapers say, "We have seen her dancing with the autumn leaves, and we saw a drift of snow in her hair."

All these things have you said of beauty, yet in truth you spoke not of her but of needs unsatisfied.

And beauty is not a need but an ecstasy.
It is not a mouth thirsting nor an empty hand
stretched forth,
but rather a heart inflamed and a soul
enchanted.
It is not the image you would see nor the song
you would hear,
but rather an image you see though you close
your eyes
and a song you hear though you shut your ears.

It is not the sap within the furrowed bark,
nor a wing attached to a claw,
but rather a garden forever in bloom
and a flock of angels forever in flight.

People of Orphalese,
beauty is life when life unveils her holy face.
But you are life and you are the veil.
Beauty is eternity gazing at itself in a mirror.
But you are eternity and you are the mirror.

SOUL OF THE DANCER

Once there came to the court of the prince of Bkerkasha a dancer with her musicians. She was admitted to the court, and she danced before the prince to the music of the lute and the flute and the zither.

She danced the dance of flames and the dance of swords and spears. She danced the dance of stars and the dance of space. And then she danced the dance of flowers in the wind.

After this, she stood before the throne of the prince and bowed her body before him.

And the prince bade her to come nearer, and he said unto her, "Beautiful woman, daughter of grace and delight, whence comes your art? And how is it that you command all the elements in your rhythms and your rhymes?"

And the dancer bowed again before the prince and she answered, "Mighty and gracious Majesty, I know not the answer to your questionings. Only this I know: The philosopher's soul dwells in the head, the poet's soul is in the heart, the singer's soul lingers about the throat, but the soul of the dancer abides in all of her body."

An Hour Devoted to Beauty and Love

One hour devoted to the pursuit of beauty and love is worth a full century of glory given by the frightened weak to the strong.

From that hour comes humanity's truth. And during that century truth sleeps between the restless arms of disturbing dreams.

In that hour the soul sees for herself the natural law, and for that century she imprisons herself behind the laws of humanity, and she is shackled with irons of oppression.

That hour was the inspiration for the Songs of Solomon, and that century was the blind power that destroyed the temple of Baalbek.

That hour was the birth of the Sermon on the Mount, and that century wrecked the castles of Palmyra and the Tower of Babylon.

That hour was the Hejira of Muhammad, and that century forgot Allah, Golgotha, and Sinai.

One hour devoted to mourning and lamenting the stolen equality of the weak is nobler than a century filled with greed and usurpation.

It is at that hour that the heart is purified by flaming sorrow and illuminated by the torch of love.

And in that century that desires for truth are buried in the bosom of the earth.

That hour is the root that must flourish.

That hour is the hour of contemplation, the hour of prayer, and the hour of a new era of good.

And that century is a life of Nero spent on self-investment taken solely from earthly substance.

This is life—portrayed on the stage for ages, recorded on earth for centuries, lived in strangeness for years, sung as a hymn for days, exalted for but an hour—but the hour is treasured by eternity as a jewel.

3

Life's Human Journey

Daily life provides the opportunity to learn about the many ways that the Greater Life expresses itself through us. The journey of human life presents its own unique twists and turns.

Your Daily Life Is Your Temple

Your daily life is your temple and your religion.
Whenever you enter into it, take with you
your all.
Take the plough and the forge and the mallet
and the lute—
the things you have fashioned in necessity or
for delight.
For in reverie you cannot rise above your
achievements
nor fall lower than your failures.
And take with you all people:
for in adoration you cannot fly higher than
their hopes
nor humble yourself lower than their despair.
And if you would know God,
be not therefore a solver of riddles.
Rather look about you and you shall see God
playing with your children.

And look into space—
you shall see God walking in the cloud,
arms outstretched in the lightning,
then descending in the rain.
You shall see God smiling in the flowers,
then rising and waving hands in the trees.

Burying Dead Selves

Once, as I was burying one of my dead selves, the gravedigger came by and said to me, "Of all those who come here to bury, you alone I like."

Said I, "You please me exceedingly, but why do you like me?"

"Because," said he, "The others come weeping and go weeping—you only come laughing and go laughing."

Giving Up a Kingdom

They told me that in a forest among the mountains lived a young man in solitude who once was a king of a vast country beyond the Two Rivers[3]. And they also said that he, of his own will, had left his throne and the land of his glory and come to dwell in the wilderness.

And I said, "I would seek that man, and learn the secret of his heart. For he who renounces a kingdom must needs be greater than a kingdom."

On that very day, I went to the forest where he dwelt. And I found him sitting under a white cypress, and in his hand he held a reed as if it were a scepter. And I greeted him even as I would greet a king. And he turned to me and said gently, "What would you in this forest of serenity? Seek you a lost self in the green shadows, or is it a homecoming in your twilight?"

And I answered, "I seek only you—for I fain would know what made you leave a kingdom for a forest."

---

3. Tigris and Euphrates.

And he said, "Brief is my story, for sudden was the bursting of the bubble. It happened thus: One day as I sat at a window in my palace, my chamberlain and an envoy from a foreign land were walking in my garden. And as they approached my window, the lord chamberlain was speaking of himself and saying, 'I am like the king. I have a thirst for strong wine and a hunger for all games of chance. And like my lord the king, I have storms of temper.' And the lord chamberlain and the envoy disappeared among the trees. But in a few minutes they returned, and this time the lord chamberlain was speaking of me, and he was saying, 'My lord the king is like myself—a good marksman—and like me he loves music and bathes thrice a day.'"

After a moment he added, "On the eve of that day, I left my palace with but my garment, for I would no longer be ruler over those who assume my vices and attribute to me their virtues."

And I said, "This is indeed a wonder, and passing strange."

And he said, "Nay, my friend, you knocked at the gate of my silences and received but a trifle.

For who would not leave a kingdom for a forest, where the seasons sing and dance ceaselessly? Many are those who have given their kingdom for less than solitude and the sweet fellowship of aloneness. Countless are the eagles who descend from the upper air to live with moles that they may know the secrets of the earth.

"There are those who renounce the kingdom of dreams that they may not seem distant from the dreamless. And those who renounce the kingdom of nakedness and cover their souls that others may not be ashamed in beholding truth uncovered and beauty unveiled.

"And greater yet than all of these are those who renounce the kingdom of sorrow that they may not seem proud and vainglorious."

Then rising, he leaned upon his reed and said, "Go now to the great city and sit at its gate and watch all those who enter into it and those who go out. And see that you find him who, though born a king, is without kingdom. And him who, though ruled in flesh, rules in spirit—though neither he nor his subjects know this.

And him also who but seems to rule yet is in truth slave of his own slaves."

After he had said these things, he smiled on me, and there were a thousand dawns upon his lips. Then he turned and walked away into the heart of the forest.

And I returned to the city, and I sat at its gate to watch the passersby, even as he had told me.

And from that day to this, numberless are the kings whose shadows have passed over me, and few are the subjects over whom my shadow passed.

POSSESSIONS

What are your possessions
but things you keep and guard
for fear you may need them tomorrow?

And tomorrow, what shall tomorrow bring
to the over-prudent dog
burying bones in the trackless sand
as it follows the pilgrims to the holy city?

And what is fear of need but need itself?
Is not dread of thirst when your well is full,
a thirst that is unquenchable?

Treasure

Dig anywhere in the earth
and you will find a treasure,
only you must dig
with the faith of a peasant.

The Value of Time

They deem me mad because
I will not sell my days for gold.
And I deem them mad because
they think my days have a price.

They spread before us their riches
of gold and silver, of ivory and ebony,
and we spread before them
our hearts and our spirits.

And yet they deem
themselves the hosts
and us the guests.

WITH SENSES CONTINUALLY MADE NEW

A philosopher describes Jesus:

When he was with us, he gazed at us and at our world with eyes of wonder, for his eyes were not veiled with the veil of years, and all that he saw was clear in the light of his youth.

Though he knew the depth of beauty, he was forever surprised by its peace and its majesty. And he stood before the earth as the first man had stood before the first day.

We whose senses have been dulled, we gaze in full daylight and yet we do not see. We would cup our ears, but we do not hear, and stretch forth our hands, but we do not touch. And though all the incense of Arabia is burned, we go our way and do not smell.

We see not the ploughman returning from his field at eventide, nor hear the shepherd's flute when he leads his flock to the fold. Nor do we stretch our arms to touch the sunset, and our nostrils hunger no longer for the roses of Sharon.

Nay, we honor no kings without kingdoms, nor hear the sound of harps save when the strings are plucked by hands. Nor do we see a child playing in our olive grove as if he were a young olive tree. And all words must needs rise from lips of flesh, or else we deem each other dumb and deaf.

In truth we gaze but do not see, and hearken but do not hear. We eat and drink but do not taste.

And there lies the difference between Jesus of Nazareth and ourselves.

His senses were all continually made new, and the world to him was always a new world.

To him the lisping of a babe was not less than the cry of all humanity, while to us it is only lisping.

To him the root of a buttercup was a longing towards God, while to us it is naught but a root.

Work Is Love

You work that you may keep pace with the earth and the soul of the earth.

For to be idle is to become a stranger unto the seasons and to step out of life's procession, which marches in majesty and proud submission towards the infinite.

When you work, you are a flute through whose heart the whispering of the hours turns to music.

When you work, you fulfill a part of earth's furthest dream, assigned to you when that dream was born.

And in keeping yourself in labor, you are in truth loving life, and to love life through labor is to be intimate with life's inmost secret.

It is not in sleep but in the overwakefulness of noontide that the wind speaks not more sweetly to the giant oaks than to the least of all the blades of grass.

And he alone is great who turns the voice of the wind into a song made sweeter by his own loving.

Work is love made visible.

Builders of Bridges

In Antioch, where the river Asi goes to meet the sea, a bridge was built to bring one half of the city nearer to the other half. It was built of large stones carried down from among the hills on the backs of the mules of Antioch.

When the bridge was finished, upon a pillar thereof was engraved in Greek and in Aramaic, "This bridge was built by King Antiochus II."

And all the people walked across the good bridge over the goodly river Asi.

And upon an evening, a youth, deemed by some a little mad, descended to the pillar where the words were engraved, and he covered over the graving with charcoal, and above it wrote,

"The stones of this bridge were brought down from the hills by the mules. In passing to and fro over it, you are riding upon the backs of the mules of Antioch, builders of this bridge."

And when the people read what the youth had written, some of them laughed and some marveled. And some said, "Ah, yes, we know who has done this. Is he not a little mad?"

But one mule said, laughing, to another mule, "Do you not remember that we did carry those stones? And yet until now it has been said that the bridge was built by King Antiochus."

Renown

Be grateful that you do not have to
live down the renown
of a father or the wealth of an uncle.
But above all be grateful that
no one will have to live down
either your renown or your wealth.

LIFE IS A PROCESSION

Life is a procession.
The slow of foot finds it too swift
and steps out.
And the swift of foot finds it too slow
and also steps out.

Song of Humanity

I was here from the
moment of the beginning,
and here I am still.
And I shall remain here
until the end of the world,
for there is no ending to
my grief-stricken being.

I roamed the infinite sky,
and soared in the ideal world,
and floated through the firmament.
But here I am,
prisoner of measurement.

I heard the teachings of Confucius.
I listened to Brahma's wisdom.
I sat by Buddha under the Tree of Knowledge.
Yet here I am,
existing with ignorance and heresy.

I was on Sinai when Jehovah approached
Moses.
I saw the Nazarene's miracles at the Jordan.
I was in Medina when Muhammad visited.
Yet here I am,
prisoner of bewilderment.

Then I witnessed the might of Babylon.
I learned of the glory of Egypt.
I viewed the warring greatness of Rome.
Yet my earlier teachings showed
the weakness and sorrow
of those achievements.

I conversed with the magicians of Ain Dour.
I debated with the priests of Assyria.
I gleaned depth from the prophets
of Palestine.
Yet I am still seeking truth.

I gathered wisdom from quiet India.
I probed the antiquity of Arabia.
I heard all that can be heard.
Yet my heart is deaf and blind.

I suffered at the hands of despotic rulers.
I suffered slavery under insane invaders.
I suffered hunger imposed by tyranny.
Yet I still possess some inner power
with which I struggle to greet each day.

My mind is filled, but my heart is empty.
My body is old, but my heart is an infant.
Perhaps in youth my heart will grow,
but I pray to grow old and reach
the moment of my return to God.
Only then will my heart fill!

I was here from the
moment of the beginning,
and here I am still.
And I shall remain here
until the end of world,
for there is no ending to
my grief-stricken being.

Singing in the Silence

Life sings in our silences
and dreams in our slumber.
Even when we are beaten and low,
life is enthroned and high.
And when we weep,
life smiles upon the day
and is free even when
we drag our chains.

Modesty

Your clothes conceal much of your beauty, yet they hide not the unbeautiful.

And though you see in garments the freedom of privacy, you may find in them a harness and a chain.

Would that you could meet the sun and the wind with more of your skin and less of your raiment. For the breath of life is in the sunlight and the hand of life is in the wind.

Some of you say, "It is the north wind who has woven the clothes to wear."

But shame was his loom, and the softening of the sinews was his thread. And when his work was done, he laughed in the forest.

Forget not that modesty is for a shield against the eye of the unclean.

And when the unclean shall be no more, what were modesty but a fetter and a fouling of the mind?

And forget not that the earth delights to feel your bare feet and the winds long to play with your hair.

Between

I am forever walking upon these shores,
betwixt the sand and the foam.
The high tide will erase my footprints,
and the wind will blow away the foam.
But the sea and the shore
will remain forever.

IGNORANCE

I am ignorant of absolute truth.
But I am humble before my ignorance
and therein lies my honor and my reward.

When You Meet a Friend

When you meet your friend on the roadside or
in the market place,
let the spirit in you move your lips and direct
your tongue.
Let the voice within your voice speak to the ear
of his ear.
For his soul will keep the truth of your heart,
as the taste of the wine is remembered
when the color is forgotten
and the vessel is no more.

STRANGERS TO LIFE

My friend, you and I shall remain
strangers unto life,
and unto one another,
and each unto ourselves,
until the day when you shall speak
and I shall listen,
deeming your voice my own voice,
and when I shall stand before you,
thinking myself standing before a mirror.

They say to me,
"Should you know yourself
you would know all people."
And I say,
"Only when I seek all people
shall I know myself."

Life Is a Resolution

Life is a resolution that accompanies youth,
and a diligence that follows maturity,
and a wisdom that pursues senility.

Knowledge is a light
enriching the warmth of life,
and all may partake who seek it out.

Humanity is a brilliant river,
singing its way and carrying with it
the mountains' secrets into
the heart of the sea.

The spirit is a sacred blue torch,
burning and devouring the dry plants,
and growing with the storm,
and illuminating the faces of the goddesses.

LONGING

He who longs the most
lives the longest.

To American Immigrants from the Middle East (1926)

I believe in you, and I believe in your destiny.

I believe that you are contributors to this new civilization.

I believe that you have inherited from your ancestors an ancient dream, a song, a prophecy, which you can proudly lay as a gift of gratitude upon the lap of America.

I believe you can say to the founders of this great nation, "Here I am, a youth, a young tree whose roots were plucked from the hills of Lebanon, yet I am deeply rooted here, and I would be fruitful."

And I believe that you can say to Abraham Lincoln, the blessed, "Jesus of Nazareth touched your lips when you spoke, and guided your hand when you wrote. And I shall uphold all that you have said and all that you have written."

I believe that you can say to Emerson and Whitman and James, "In my veins runs the blood of the poets and wise men of old, and it is my desire to come to you and receive, but I shall not come with empty hands."

I believe that even as your ancestors came to this land to produce riches, you were born here to produce riches by intelligence, by labor.

And I believe that it is in you to be good citizens.

And what is it to be a good citizen?

It is to acknowledge the other person's rights before asserting your own, but always to be conscious of your own.

It is to be free in thought and deed, but it is to know that your freedom is subject to the other person's freedom.

It is to create the useful and the beautiful with your own hands, and to admire what others have created in love and with faith.

It is to produce wealth by labor and only by labor, and to spend less than you have produced, so that your children may not be dependent on the state for support when you are no more.

It is to stand before the towers of New York, Washington, Chicago, and San Francisco saying in your heart, "I am the descendant of a people that built Damascus and Byblos, and Tyre and Sidon and Antioch, and now I am here to build with you, and with a will."

It is to be proud of being an American, but it is also to be proud that your fathers and mothers came from a land upon which God laid his gracious hand and raised his messengers.

Young Americans of Syrian origin, I believe in you.

4

Seasons of Life

Life pulses in the rhythms that we find in the revolutions of day and night, the changing of the seasons, and the beating of our own hearts.

Changing with the Seasons

The mountains, trees, and rivers change their appearance with the vicissitudes of times and seasons, as one changes with one's experiences and emotions.

The lofty poplar that resembles a bride in the daytime will look like a column of smoke in the evening.

The huge rock that stands impregnable at noon will appear to be a miserable pauper at night, with earth for its bed and the sky for its cover.

And the rivulet that we see glittering in the morning and hear singing the hymn of eternity will, in the evening, turn to a stream of tears wailing like a mother bereft of her child.

And Lebanon, which had looked dignified a week before, when the moon was full and our spirits were happy, looked sorrowful and lonesome that night.

No Miracles Beyond the Seasons

An astronomer speaks of Jesus:

You question me concerning the miracles of Jesus.

Every thousand thousand years, the sun and the moon and this earth and all her sister planets meet in a straight line, and they confer for a moment together.

Then they slowly disperse and await the passing of another thousand thousand years.

There are no miracles beyond the seasons, yet you and I do not know all the seasons.

And what if a season shall be made manifest in the shape of a human being?

In Jesus, the elements of our bodies and our dreams came together according to law. All that was timeless before him became time-full in him.

They say he gave sight to the blind and walking to the paralyzed, and that he drove devils out of the mad.

Perchance blindness is but a dark thought that can be overcome by a burning thought.

Perchance a withered limb is but idleness that can be quickened by energy.

And perhaps the devils, these restless elements in our lives, are driven out by the angels of peace and serenity.

They say he raised the dead to life. If you can tell me what is death, then I will tell you what is life.

In a field, I have watched an acorn, a thing so still and seemingly useless. And in the spring, I have seen that acorn take roots and rise—the beginning of an oak tree—towards the sun.

Surely you would deem this a miracle, yet that miracle is wrought a thousand thousand times in the drowsiness of every autumn and the passion of every spring.

Why shall it not be wrought in the heart of a human being? Shall not the seasons meet in the hand or upon the lips of one anointed?

If our God has given to earth the art to nestle seed whilst the seed is seemingly dead, why shall he not give to the heart of a human being the art to breathe life into another heart, even a heart seemingly dead?

I have spoken of these miracles that I deem but little beside the greater miracle, which is the man himself, the Wayfarer, the man who turned my dross into gold, who taught me how to love those who hate me, and in so doing brought me comfort and gave sweet dreams to my sleep.

This is the miracle in my own life.

My soul was blind, my soul was lame. I was possessed by restless spirits, and I was dead.

But now I see clearly, and I walk erect. I am at peace, and I live to witness and proclaim my own being every hour of the day.

And I am not one of his followers. I am but an old astronomer who visits the fields of space once a season and who would be heedful of the law and the miracles thereof.

And I am at the twilight of my time, but whenever I would seek its dawning, I seek the youth of Jesus.

And forever shall age seek youth.

In me now, it is knowledge that is seeking vision.

Youth and Knowledge

You cannot have youth
and the knowledge of it
at the same time.
For youth is too busy living
to know,
and knowledge is too busy
seeking itself
to live.

Seasons

What are the seasons of the years
save your own thoughts changing?
Spring is an awakening in your breast,
and summer but a recognition of your own
  fruitfulness.
Is not autumn the ancient in you singing
  a lullaby
to that which is still a child in your being?
And what, I ask you, is winter save sleep
big with the dreams
of all the other seasons?

Autumn and Spring

In the autumn, I gathered all my sorrows and buried them in my garden.

And when April returned and spring came to wed the earth, there grew in my garden beautiful flowers unlike all other flowers.

And my neighbors came to behold them, and they all said to me,

"When autumn comes again, at seeding time, will you not give us of the seeds of these flowers that we may have them in our gardens?"

TIME

Of time you would make a stream
upon whose bank you would sit
and watch its flowing.

Yet the timeless in you
is aware of life's timelessness
and knows that yesterday
is but today's memory
and tomorrow is today's dream.
And that that which sings and
contemplates in you is still dwelling
within the bounds of that first moment
that scattered the stars into space.

But if in your thought
you must measure time into seasons,
let each season encircle all the other seasons,
and let today embrace
the past with remembrance
and the future with longing.

All Your Hours Are Wings

Is not religion all deeds and all reflection,
and that which is neither deed nor reflection,
but a wonder and a surprise
ever springing in the soul,
even while the hands hew the stone
or tend the loom?

Who can separate faith from actions,
or belief from one's occupations?
Who can spread one's hours before one, saying,
"This for God and this for myself.
This for my soul,
and this other for my body?"

All your hours are wings
that beat through space
from self to self.

Be Dark

When night comes, and you too are dark,
lie down and be dark with a will.
And when morning comes, and you are still
dark,
stand up and say to the day with a will,
"I am still dark."
It is stupid to play a role with the night and
the day.
They would both laugh at you.

Day and Night

You grow in sleep and live your fuller life in your dreaming.

For all your days are spent in thanksgiving for that which you have received in the stillness of the night.

Oftentimes you think and speak of night as the season of rest, yet in truth night is the season of seeking and finding.

The day gives unto you the power of knowledge and teaches your fingers to become versed in the art of receiving.

But it is night that leads you to the treasure house of Life.

The sun teaches to all things that grow their longing for the light.

But it is night that raises them to the stars.

SHELL-LIFE

Perhaps the sea's
definition of a shell
is the pearl.
Perhaps time's
definition of coal
is the diamond.

Tides of Breath

That which seems most feeble and bewildered in you is the strongest and most determined.

Is it not your breath that has erected and hardened the structure of your bones?

Could you but see the tides of that breath, you would cease to see all else.

Shoreless Without a Self

It was but yesterday that
you were moving with the moving sea,
and you were shoreless and without a self.

Then the wind, the breath of Life,
wove you, a veil of light on her face.
Then her hand gathered you
and gave you form,
and with a head held high
you sought the heights.

But the sea followed after you,
and her song is still with you.

Finding Fault

If I were you
I would not find fault
with the sea
at low tide.

Every Year I Had Waited for Spring . . .

Rachel, a woman disciple of Jesus speaks:

I often wonder whether Jesus was a man of flesh and blood like ourselves, or a thought without a body, in the mind, or an idea that visits the vision of humanity.

Often it seems to me that he was but a dream dreamed by countless men and women at the same time in a sleep deeper than sleep and a dawn more serene than all dawns.

And it seems that, in relating the dream, one to another, we began to deem it a reality that had indeed come to pass. And in giving it a body of our fancy and a voice of our longing we made it a substance of our own substance.

But in truth he was not a dream. We knew him for three years and beheld him with our open eyes in the high tide of noon.

We touched his hands, and we followed him from one place to another. We heard his discourses and witnessed his deeds. Think you that we were a thought seeking after more thought, or a dream in the region of dreams?

Great events always seem alien to our daily lives, though their nature may be rooted in our nature. But though they appear sudden in their coming and sudden in their passing, their true span is for years and for generations.

Jesus of Nazareth was himself the Great Event. That man whose father and mother and brothers we know was himself a miracle wrought in Judea. Yea, all his own miracles, if placed at his feet, would not rise to the height of his ankles.

And all the rivers of all the years shall not carry away our remembrance of him.

He was a mountain burning in the night, yet he was a soft glow beyond the hills. He was a tempest in the sky, yet he was a murmur in the mist of daybreak.

He was a torrent pouring from the heights to the plains to destroy all things in its path. And he was like the laughter of children.

Every year I had waited for spring to visit this valley. I had waited for the lilies and the cyclamen, and then every year my soul had been saddened within me. For ever I longed to rejoice with the spring, yet I could not.

But when Jesus came to my seasons he was indeed a spring, and in him was the promise of all the years to come. He filled my heart with joy, and like the violets I grew, a shy thing, in the light of his coming.

And now the changing seasons of worlds not yet ours shall not erase his loveliness from this our world.

Nay, Jesus was not a phantom, nor a conception of the poets. He was man like yourself and myself. But only to sight and touch and hearing. In all other ways, he was unlike us.

He was a man of joy, and it was upon the path of joy that he met the sorrows of everyone. And it was from the high roofs of his sorrows that he beheld the joy of everyone.

He saw visions that we did not see and heard voices that we did not hear. And he spoke as if to invisible multitudes, and ofttimes he spoke through us to races yet unborn.

And Jesus was often alone. He was among us yet not one with us. He was upon the earth, yet he was of the sky. And only in our aloneness may we visit the land of his aloneness.

He loved us with tender love. His heart was a winepress. You and I could approach with a cup and drink therefrom.

One thing I did not use to understand in Jesus: he would make merry with his listeners. He would tell jests and play upon words, and laugh with all the fullness of his heart, even when there were distances in his eyes and sadness in his voice. But I understand now.

I often think of the earth as a woman heavy with her first child. When Jesus was born, he was the first child. And when he died, he was the first man to die.

For did it not appear to you that the earth was stilled on that dark Friday, and the heavens were at war with the heavens?

And felt you not when his face disappeared from our sight as if we were naught but memories in the mist?

5

Paradoxical Life

In life's contradictions and paradoxes, we discover the unity of all Life, a unity reflected in the soul's experience of oneness.

Life Comes Walking

And Life is veiled and hidden, even as your Greater Self is hidden and veiled.

Yet when Life speaks, all the winds become words.

And when she speaks again, the smiles upon your lips and the tears in your eyes turn also into words.

When she sings, the deaf hear and are held.

And when she comes walking, the sightless behold her and are amazed and follow her in wonder and astonishment.

Talk

In truth we talk only to ourselves,
but sometimes we talk loud enough
that others may hear us.

A Tale of Two Tales

Once upon an evening, a man and a woman found themselves together in a stagecoach. They had met before.

The man was a poet, and as he sat beside the woman, he sought to amuse her with stories, some that were of his own weaving, and some that were not his own.

But even while he was speaking, the lady went to sleep. Then suddenly the coach lurched, and she awoke, and she said, "I admire your interpretation of the story of Jonah and the whale."

And the poet said, "But madame, I have been telling you a story of my own about a butterfly and a white rose, and how they behaved the one to the other!"

Confession

Should we all confess our sins to one another,
we would all laugh at one another
for our lack of originality.

Should we all reveal our virtues,
we would also laugh
for the same cause.

Yesterday and Today

The gold-hoarder walked in his palace park, and with him walked his troubles. And over his head hovered worries as a vulture hovers over a carcass, until he reached a beautiful lake surrounded by magnificent marble statuary.

He sat there pondering the water that poured from the mouths of the statues, like thoughts flowing freely from a lover's imagination. And he contemplated heavily his palace, which stood upon a knoll like a birthmark upon the cheek of a maiden.

His fancy revealed to him the pages of his life's drama, which he read with falling tears that veiled his eyes and prevented him from viewing humanity's feeble additions to nature.

He looked back with piercing regret to the images of his early life, woven into pattern by the gods, until he could no longer control his anguish. He said aloud:

"Yesterday, I was grazing my sheep in the green valley, enjoying my existence, sounding my flute, and holding my head high. Today I am a prisoner of greed. Gold leads into gold, then into restlessness, and finally into crushing misery.

"Yesterday, I was like a singing bird, soaring freely here and there in the fields. Today, I am a slave to fickle wealth, society's rules, city's customs, purchased friends, and pleasing the people by conforming to the strange and narrow laws of humanity. I was born to be free and enjoy the bounty of life, but I find myself like a beast of burden so heavily laden with gold that its back is breaking.

"Where are the spacious plains, the singing brooks, the pure breeze, the closeness of nature? Where is my deity? I have lost all! Naught remains save loneliness that saddens me, gold that ridicules me, slaves who curse me to my back, and a palace that I have erected as a tomb for my happiness, and in whose greatness I have lost my heart.

"Yesterday, I roamed the prairies and the hills together with the Bedouin's daughter. Virtue was our companion, love our delight, and the moon our guardian. Today, I am among women with shallow beauty who sell themselves for gold and diamonds.

"Yesterday, I was carefree, sharing with the shepherds all the joy of life—eating, playing, working, singing, and dancing together to the music of the heart's truth. Today, I find myself among the people like a frightened lamb among the wolves. As I walk in the roads, they gaze at me with hateful eyes and point at me with scorn and jealousy, and as I steal through the park, I see frowning faces all about me.

"Yesterday, I was rich in happiness and today I am poor in gold.

"Yesterday I was a happy shepherd looking upon his herd as a merciful king looks with pleasure upon his contented subjects. Today, I am a slave standing before my wealth, my wealth that robbed me of the beauty of life I once knew.

"Forgive me, my Judge! I did not know that riches would put my life into fragments and lead me into the dungeons of harshness and stupidity. What I thought was glory is naught but an eternal inferno."

He gathered himself wearily and walked slowly toward the palace, sighing and repeating, "Is this what people call wealth? Is this the god I am serving and worshipping? Is this what I seek of the earth? Why can I not trade it for one particle of contentment? Who would sell me one beautiful thought for a ton of gold? Who would give me one moment of love for a handful of gems? Who would grant me an eye that can see others' hearts, and take all in my coffers in barter?"

As he reached the palace gates, he turned and looked toward the city as Jeremiah gazed toward Jerusalem. He raised his arms in woeful lament and shouted:

"Oh, people of the noisome city, who are living in darkness, hastening toward misery, preaching falsehood, and speaking with stupidity! Until when shall you remain ignorant? Until when shall you abide in the filth of life and continue to desert its gardens? Why wear your tattered robes of narrowness while the silk raiment of nature's beauty is fashioned for you? The lamp of wisdom is dimming; it is time to furnish it with oil. The house of true fortune is being destroyed. It is time to rebuild it and guard it. The thieves of ignorance have stolen the treasure of your peace. It is time to retake it!"

At that moment, a poor man stood before him and stretched forth his hand for alms. As he looked at the beggar, his lips parted, his eyes brightened with a softness, and his face radiated kindness. It was as if the yesterday he had lamented by the lake had come to greet him. He embraced the pauper with affection and filled his hands with gold. And with a voice sincere with the sweetness of love, he said, "Come back tomorrow and bring with you your fellow sufferers. All your possessions will be restored."

He entered his palace, saying, "Everything in life is good, even gold, for it teaches a lesson.

"Money is like a stringed instrument. He who does not know how to use it properly will hear only discordant music.

"Money is like love. It kills slowly and painfully the one who withholds it, and it enlivens the one who turns it upon his fellow human beings."

Gifts of the Earth

To you the earth yields her fruit, and you shall not want if you but know how to fill your hands.

It is in exchanging the gifts of the earth that you shall find abundance and be satisfied.

Yet unless the exchange be in love and kindly justice, it will but lead some to greed and others to hunger.

GIVING AND GAINING

You are good when you strive to give of yourself.

Yet you are not evil when you seek gain for yourself.

For when you strive for gain, you are but a root that clings to the earth and sucks at her breast.

Surely the fruit cannot say to the root, "Be like me, ripe and full and ever giving of your abundance."

For to the fruit, giving is a need, as receiving is a need to the root.

High and Low

But I say that even as the holy and the righteous cannot rise beyond the highest that is in each one of you, so the wicked and the weak cannot fall lower than the lowest that is in you also.

And as a single leaf turns not yellow but with the silent knowledge of the whole tree, so the wrongdoer cannot do wrong without the hidden will of you all.

Like a procession, you walk together towards your godself.

You are the way and the wayfarers.

SEEKING

They say to me, "A bird in the hand is worth ten in the bush."

But I say, "A bird and a feather in the bush are worth more than ten birds in the hand."

Your seeking after that feather is life with winged feet—nay, it is life itself.

FREEDOM

And an orator said, "Speak to us of freedom."

And he answered:

At the city gate and by your fireside, I have seen you prostrate yourself and worship your own freedom, even as slaves humble themselves before a tyrant and praise him, though he slays them.

Aye, in the grove of the temple and in the shadow of the citadel, I have seen the freest among you wear their freedom as a yoke and a handcuff.

And my heart bled within me, for you can only be free when even the desire of seeking freedom becomes a harness to you, and when you cease to speak of freedom as a goal and a fulfilment.

You shall be free indeed when your days are not without a care nor your nights without a want and a grief, but rather when these things girdle your life and yet you rise above them, naked and unbound.

And how shall you rise beyond your days and nights unless you break the chains that you, at the dawn of your understanding, have fastened around your noon hour?

In truth, that which you call freedom is the strongest of these chains, though its links glitter in the sun and dazzle the eyes.

And what is it but fragments of your own self you would discard that you may become free?

If it is an unjust law you would abolish, that law was written with your own hand upon your own forehead.

You cannot erase it by burning your law books nor by washing the foreheads of your judges, though you pour the sea upon them.

And if it is a despot you would dethrone, see first that his throne erected within you is destroyed.

For how can a tyrant rule the free and the proud, but for a tyranny in their own freedom and a shame in their own pride?

And if it is a care you would cast off, that care has been chosen by you rather than imposed upon you.

And if it is a fear you would dispel, the seat of that fear is in your heart and not in the hand of the feared.

Verily, all things move within your being in constant half embrace, the desired and the dreaded, the repugnant and the cherished, the pursued and that which you would escape.

These things move within you as lights and shadows in pairs that cling.

And when the shadow fades and is no more, the light that lingers becomes a shadow to another light.

And thus your freedom when it loses its fetters becomes itself the fetter of a greater freedom.

LIMITS

When you reach the end
of what you should know,
you will be at the beginning
of what you should sense.

Owl Eyes

The owl whose night-bound eyes
are blind unto the day
cannot unveil the mystery of light.
If you would indeed behold the spirit of death,
open your heart wide to the body of life.
For life and death are one,
even as the river and the sea are one.

VOICES

I said to Life,
"I would hear Death speak."
And Life raised her voice a little higher and said,
"You hear him now."

Ocean and Foam

You have been told that, even like a chain, you are as weak as your weakest link.

This is but half the truth.

You are also as strong as your strongest link.

To measure you by your smallest deed is to reckon the power of ocean by the frailty of its foam.

To judge you by your failures is to cast blame upon the seasons for their inconsistency.

Blessing Darkness

Is it not a dream that none of you
remember having dreamt
that built your city and
fashioned all there is in it?

If you could hear the whispering of the dream,
you would hear no other sound.
But you do not see,
nor do you hear,
and it is well.

The veil that clouds your eyes shall be lifted
by the hands that wove it,
and the clay that fills your ears shall be pierced
by those fingers that kneaded it.
And you shall see.
And you shall hear.

Yet you shall not deplore
having known blindness,
nor regret having been deaf.
For you shall know
the hidden purposes in all things,
and you shall bless darkness
as you would bless light.

Agreement

Once every hundred years, Jesus of Nazareth
meets Jesus of the Christian
in a garden among the hills of Lebanon.
And they talk long.
And each time, Jesus of Nazareth goes away
saying to Jesus of the Christian,
"My friend, I fear we shall never, never agree."

Jesus and Pan

The voice of Sarkis, an old Greek shepherd, called the Madman:

In a dream, I saw Jesus and my God Pan sitting together in the heart of the forest.

They laughed at each other's speech, with the brook that ran near them, and the laughter of Jesus was the merrier. And they conversed long.

Pan spoke of earth and her secrets, and of his hoofed brothers and his horned sisters, and of dreams. And he spoke of roots and their nestlings, and of the sap that wakes and rises and sings to summer.

And Jesus told of the young shoots in the forest, and of flowers and fruit, and the seed that they shall bear in a season not yet come.

He spoke of birds in space and their singing in the upper world. And he told of white harts in the desert wherein God shepherds them.

And Pan was pleased with the speech of the new God, and his nostrils quivered.

And in the same dream, I beheld Pan and Jesus grow quiet and still in the stillness of the green shadows.

And then Pan took his reeds and played to Jesus.

The trees were shaken and the ferns trembled, and there was a fear upon me.

And Jesus said, "Good brother, you have the glade and the rocky height in your reeds."

Then Pan gave the reeds to Jesus and said, "You play now. It is your turn."

And Jesus said, "These reeds are too many for my mouth. I have this flute."

And he took his flute and he played. And I heard the sound of rain in the leaves, and the singing of streams among the hills, and the falling of snow on the mountaintop.

The pulse of my heart, which had once beaten with the wind, was restored again to the wind, and all the waves of my yesterdays were upon my shore, and I was again Sarkis the shepherd. And the flute of Jesus became the pipes of countless shepherds calling to countless flocks.

Then Pan said to Jesus, "Your youth is more kin to the reed than my years. And long ere this in my stillness I have heard your song and the murmur of your name.

"Your name has a goodly sound. Well shall it rise with the sap to the branches, and well shall it run with the hoofs among the hills.

"And it is not strange to me, though my father called me not by that name. It was your flute that brought it back to my memory.

"And now let us play our reeds together."

And they played together.

And their music smote heaven and earth, and a terror struck all living things.

I heard the bellow of beasts and the hunger of the forest.

And I heard the cry of lonely men, and the plaint of those who long for what they know not.

I heard the sighing of the maiden for her lover, and the panting of the luckless hunter for his prey.

And then there came peace into their music, and the heavens and the earth sang together.

All this I saw in my dream, and all this I heard.

6

The Life of the Soul

Awake or asleep, dreaming or in everyday life, the Greater Self is always living through us, leading us further in Love's procession.

Resurrection of Life

The voice of Nicodemus the Poet:

I know these moles that dig paths to nowhere.

Are they not the ones who accuse Jesus of glorifying himself in that he said to the multitude, "I am the path and the gate to salvation," and even called himself the life and the resurrection.

But Jesus was not claiming more than the month of May claims in her high tide.

A Fragment

It was but yesterday I thought myself a fragment quivering without rhythm in the sphere of life.

Now I know that I am the sphere, and all life in rhythmic fragments moves within me.

They say to me in their awakening,

"You and the world you live in are but a grain of sand upon the infinite shore of an infinite sea."

And in my dream I say to them,

"I am the infinite sea, and all worlds are but grains of sand upon my shore.

The Greater Sea

My soul and I went down to the great sea to bathe. And when we reached the shore, we went about looking for a hidden and lonely place.

But as we walked, we saw a man sitting on a grey rock taking pinches of salt from a bag and throwing them into the sea.

"This is the pessimist," said my soul. "Let us leave this place. We cannot bathe here."

We walked on until we reached an inlet. There we saw standing on a white rock a man holding a bejewelled box, from which he took sugar and threw it into the sea.

"And this is the optimist," said my soul. "And he too must not see our naked bodies."

Further on we walked. And on a beach we saw a man picking up dead fish and tenderly putting them back into the water.

"And we cannot bathe before him," said my soul. "He is the humane philanthropist."

And we passed on.

Then we came where we saw a man tracing his shadow on the sand. Great waves came and erased it. But he went on tracing it again and again.

"He is the mystic," said my soul. "Let us leave him."

And we walked on, till in a quiet cove we saw a man scooping up the foam and putting it into an alabaster bowl.

"He is the idealist," said my soul. "Surely he must not see our nudity."

And on we walked.

Suddenly we heard a voice crying, "This is the sea. This is the deep sea. This is the vast and mighty sea." And when we reached the voice, it was a man whose back was turned to the sea, and at his ear he held a shell, listening to its murmur.

And my soul said, "Let us pass on. He is the realist, who turns his back on the whole he cannot grasp, and busies himself with a fragment."

So we passed on.

And in a weedy place among the rocks was a man with his head buried in the sand. And I said to my soul, "We can bathe here, for he cannot see us."

"Nay," said my soul, "for he is the most deadly of them all. He is the puritan."

Then a great sadness came over the face of my soul and into her voice.

"Let us go hence," she said, "for there is no lonely, hidden place where we can bathe. I would not have this wind lift my golden hair, or bare my white bosom in this air, or let the light disclose my sacred nakedness."

Then we left that sea to seek the Greater Sea.

Truth Is Like the Stars

The true light is that which emanates from within a person.

It reveals the secrets of the heart to the soul, making it happy and contented with life.

Truth is like the stars. It does not appear except from behind obscurity of the night.

Truth is like all beautiful things in the world. It does not disclose its desirability except to those who first feel the influence of falsehood.

Truth is a deep kindness that teaches us to be content in our everyday life and share with people the same happiness.

Have Mercy on Me, My Soul

Why are you weeping, my Soul?
Knowest thou my weakness?
Thy tears strike sharp and injure,
for I know not my wrong.
Until when shalt thou cry?
I have naught but human words
to interpret your dreams,
your desires, and your instructions.

Look upon me, my Soul.
I have consumed my full life
heeding your teachings.
Think of how I suffer!
I have exhausted my life following you.

My heart was glorying upon the throne,
but is now yoked in slavery.
My patience was a companion,
but now contends against me.
My youth was my hope,
but now reprimands my neglect.

Why, my Soul, are you all-demanding?
I have denied myself pleasure
and deserted the joy of life
following the course that
you impelled me to pursue.
Be just to me,
or call Death to unshackle me,
for justice is your glory.

Have mercy on me, my Soul.
You have laden me with Love
until I cannot carry my burden.
You and Love are inseparable might.
Substance and I are inseparable weakness.
Will e'er the struggle cease
between the strong and the weak?

Have mercy on me, my Soul.
You have shown me Fortune beyond my grasp.
You and Fortune abide on the mountaintop.
Misery and I are abandoned together
in the pit of the valley.
Will e'er the mountain and the valley unite?

Have mercy on me, my Soul.
You have shown me Beauty
but then concealed her.
You and Beauty live in the light.
Ignorance and I are bound together in the dark.
Will e'er the light invade darkness?

Your delight comes with the Ending,
and you revel now in anticipation.
But this body suffers with life
while in life.
This, my Soul, is perplexing.

You are hastening toward eternity,
but this body goes slowly toward perishment.
You do not wait for him,
and he cannot go quickly.
This, my Soul, is sadness.

You ascend high through heaven's attraction,
but this body falls by earth's gravity.
You do not console him,
and he does not appreciate you.
This, my Soul, is misery.

You are rich in wisdom,
but this body is poor in understanding.
You do not compromise,
and he does not obey.
This, my Soul, is extreme suffering.

In the silence of the night, you visit the Beloved
and enjoy the sweetness of his presence.
This body ever remains
the bitter victim of hope and separation.
This, my Soul, is agonizing torture.

Have mercy on me, my Soul!

Trust the Dreams

In the depth of your hopes and desires
lies your silent knowledge of the beyond.
And like seeds dreaming beneath the snow
your heart dreams of spring.

Trust the dreams,
for in them is hidden
the gate to eternity.

The Greater Self

This came to pass.

After the coronation of Nufsibaal, King of Byblos, he retired to his bedchamber—the very room that the three hermit-magicians of the mountains had built for him.

He took off his crown and his royal raiment, and stood in the center of the room thinking of himself, now the all-powerful ruler of Byblos.

Suddenly he turned, and he saw stepping out of the silver mirror that his mother had given him a naked man.

The king was startled, and he cried out to the man, "What would you?"

And the naked man answered, "Naught but this: Why have they crowned you king?"

And the king answered, "Because I am the noblest man in the land."

Then the naked man said, "If you were still more noble, you would not be king."

And the king said, "Because I am the mightiest man in the land they crowned me."

And the naked man said, "If you were mightier yet, you would not be king."

Then the king said, "Because I am the wisest man they crowned me king."

And the naked man said, "If you were still wiser you would not choose to be king."

Then the king fell to the floor and wept bitterly.

The naked man looked down upon him. Then he took up the crown and with tenderness replaced it upon the king's bent head.

And the naked man, gazing lovingly upon the king, entered into the mirror.

And the king roused, and straightway he looked into the mirror. And he saw there but himself crowned.

Rising

When you long for blessings
that you may not name,
and when you grieve
knowing not the cause,
then indeed you are growing
with all things that grow,
and rising toward your Greater Self.

Children of Space

Verily, the lust for comfort murders the passion of the soul, and then walks grinning in the funeral.

But you, children of space, you restless in rest, you shall not be trapped nor tamed.

Your house shall be not an anchor but a mast.

It shall not be a glistening film that covers a wound, but an eyelid that guards the eye.

You shall not fold your wings that you may pass through doors, nor bend your heads that they strike not against a ceiling, nor fear to breathe lest walls should crack and fall down.

You shall not dwell in tombs made by the dead for the living.

And though of magnificence and splendor, your house shall not hold your secret nor shelter your longing.

For that which is boundless in you abides in the mansion of the sky, whose door is the morning mist, and whose windows are the songs and the silences of night.

LEAVE ME, MY BLAMER

Leave me, my Blamer,
for the sake of the love that unites your soul
with that of your beloved one.
For the sake of that which joins
spirit with mother's affection,
and ties your heart with filial love.
Go, and leave me to my own weeping heart.

Let me sail in the ocean of my dreams.
Wait until tomorrow comes,
for tomorrow is free to do with me as it wishes.
Your flaying is naught but shadow
that walks with the spirit
to the tomb of abashment,
and shows her the cold, solid earth.

I have a little heart within me
and I like to bring it out of its prison
and carry it on the palm of my hand
to examine it in depth and extract its secret.
Aim not your arrows at it,
lest it takes fright and vanish 'ere

it pours the secret's blood
as a sacrifice on the altar of its own faith,
given it by Deity when he
fashioned it of love and beauty.

The sun is rising and the nightingale is singing,
and the myrtle is breathing its fragrance into
    space.
I want to free myself from the quilted slumber
    of wrong.
Do not detain me, my Blamer!

Cavil me not by mention
of the lions of the forest
or the snakes of the valley,
for my soul knows no fear of earth
and accepts no warning of evil
before evil comes.

Advise me not, my Blamer,
for calamities have opened my heart,
and tears have cleansed my eyes,

and errors have taught me
the language of the hearts.

Talk not of banishment
for conscience is my judge,
and it will justify me and protect me
if I am innocent,
and will deny me of life
if I am a criminal.

Love's procession is moving.
Beauty is waving her banner.
Youth is sounding the trumpet of joy.
Disturb not my contrition, my Blamer.
Let me walk,
for the path is rich with roses and mint,
and the air is scented with cleanliness.

Relate not the tales of wealth and greatness,
for my soul is rich with bounty
and great with God's glory.

Speak not of peoples and laws and kingdoms,
for the whole earth is my birthplace
and all people are my brothers and sisters.

Go from me,
for you are taking away life—
offering repentance and
bringing needless words.

The Forerunner

You are your own forerunner, and the towers you have built are but the foundation of your Giant Self.

And that Self too shall be a foundation.

And I too am my own forerunner, for the long shadow stretching before me at sunrise shall gather under my feet at the noon hour.

Yet another sunrise shall lay another shadow before me, and that also shall be gathered at another noon.

Always have we been our own forerunners, and always shall we be. And all that we have gathered and shall gather shall be but seeds for fields yet unploughed. We are the fields and those who plough, the gatherers and the gathered.

When you were a wandering desire in the mist, I too was there, a wandering desire. Then we sought one another, and out of our eagerness dreams were born. And dreams were time limitless, and dreams were space without measure.

And when you were a silent word upon Life's quivering lips, I too was there, another silent word. Then Life uttered us and we came down the years throbbing with memories of yesterday and with longing for tomorrow, for yesterday was death conquered and tomorrow was birth pursued.

And now we are in God's hands. You are a sun in his right hand and I an earth in his left hand. Yet you are not more, shining, than I, shone upon.

And we, sun and earth, are but the beginning of a greater sun and a greater earth. And always shall we be the beginning.

You are your own forerunner, you—the stranger passing by the gate of my garden.

And I too am my own forerunner, though I sit in the shadows of my trees and seem motionless.

Walk Facing the Sun

You who walk facing the sun,
what images drawn on the earth can hold you?
You who travel with the wind,
what weather vane shall direct your course?
What human law shall bind you
if you break your yoke,
but upon no one's prison door?
What laws shall you fear if you dance,
but stumble against no one's iron chains?
And who shall bring you to judgment
if you tear off your garment
yet leave it in no one's path?
People of Orphalese,
you can muffle the drum,
and you can loosen the strings of the lyre,
but who shall command
the skylark not to sing?

Soul's Dewdrop

The image of the morning sun in a dewdrop is not less than the sun.

The reflection of life in your soul is not less than life.

The dewdrop mirrors the light because it is one with light, and you reflect life because you and life are one.

The dewdrop rounding its sphere in the dusk of the lily is not unlike yourself gathering your soul in the heart of God.

Roots Between

You are but roots
between the dark sod
and the moving heavens.
And oftentimes have I seen you
rising to dance with the light,
but I have also seen you shy.
All roots are shy.
They have hidden their hearts so long
that they know not what to
do with their hearts.

Self Is a Sea

Your hearts know in silence the secrets of the days and the nights.

But your ears thirst for the sound of your heart's knowledge. You would know in words that which you have always known in thought. You would touch with your fingers the naked body of your dreams. And it is well you should.

The hidden wellspring of your soul must needs rise and run murmuring to the sea. And the treasure of your infinite depths would be revealed to your eyes. But let there be no scales to weigh your unknown treasure. And seek not the depths of your knowledge with staff or sounding line. For self is a sea boundless and measureless.

Say not, "I have found the truth," but rather, "I have found a truth."

Say not, "I have found the path of the soul." Say rather, "I have met the soul walking upon my path."

For the soul walks upon all paths.

The soul walks not upon a line, neither does it grow like a reed. The soul unfolds itself like a lotus of countless petals.

The Longing of the Giant Self

Pity that the stags cannot teach swiftness to the turtles.

In your longing for your Giant Self lies your goodness, and that longing is in all of you.

But in some of you that longing is a torrent rushing with might to the sea, carrying the secrets of the hillsides and the songs of the forest.

And in others it is a flat stream that loses itself in angles and bends and lingers before it reaches the shore.

But let not the one who longs much say to the one who longs little, "Wherefore are you slow and halting?"

Angels and Devils

I too am visited
by angels and devils,
but I get rid of them.

When it is an angel,
I pray an old prayer
and he is bored.

When it is a devil,
I commit an old sin
and he passes me by.

Blessed Mountain

You may have heard of
the Blessed Mountain.
It is the highest mountain in our world.

Should you reach the summit
you would have only one desire,
and that to descend and
be with those who dwell
in the deepest valley.

That is why it is called
the Blessed Mountain.

Song of the Soul

In the depth of my soul
there is a wordless song,
a song that lives
in the seed of my heart.

It refuses to melt
with ink on parchment.
It engulfs my affection
in a transparent cloak and flows,
but not upon my lips.

How can I sigh it?
I fear it may mingle with earthly ether.
To whom shall I sing it?
It dwells in the house of my soul
in fear of harsh ears.

When I look into my inner eyes,
I see the shadow of its shadow.
When I touch my fingertips,
I feel its vibrations.

The deeds of my hands
heed its presence,
as a lake must reflect
the glittering stars.

My tears reveal it,
as bright drops of dew
reveal the secret
of a withering rose.

It is a song composed
by contemplation
and published by silence
and shunned by clamor
and folded by truth
and repeated by dreams
and understood by love
and hidden by awakening
and sung by the soul.

It is the song of love.
What Cain or Esau could sing it?

It is more fragrant than jasmine.
What voice could enslave it?

It is as heart-bound
as a virgin's secret.
What string could quiver it?

Who dares unite the roar of the sea
and the singing of the nightingale?

Who dares compare the shrieking tempest
to the sigh of an infant?

Who dares speak aloud the words
intended for the heart to speak?

What human dares
sing in voice
the song of God?

Sources of the Selections

Spirits Rebellious (1908) SR
The Broken Wings (1912) BW
A Tear and a Smile (1914) TS
The Procession (1918) TP
The Madman (1918) M
"My Countrymen" (1920s) MC
The Forerunner (1920) F
The Prophet (1923) P
Sand and Foam (1926) SF
"To Young Americans of Syrian Origin" (1926) YA
Jesus The Son of Man (1928) JSM
The Wanderer (1932) W
The Garden of the Prophet (1933) GP

Selection Notes

Listening to Nature's Life

The Law of Nature. SR
Said a Blade of Grass. M
Three Dogs. W
Shadows. M
Song of the Rain. TS
A Hyena and a Crocodile. W
Two Oysters. W
Trees Are Poems. SF
The Red Earth. W
The Full Moon. W
The Supreme Ant. M
The Pomegranate. M
Solitude. SF
Living Water. P
Other Seas. F
The River. W
Contentment and Thrift. SF
The Lotus-Heart. JSM. "Jonathan: Among the Water-lilies."

The Shadow. W

The Serpent and the Lark. F. "The Scholar and the Poet"

Frogs: On the Nature of Disturbance. W

Song of the Flower. TS

Spring in Lebanon. BW

Beauty and the Song of Life

Life's Purpose. SF

Singing. SF

Secrets of the Beauty of Life. SR. "Khalil the Heretic."

The Poet. TS

Art and Life. F

Pleasure Is a Freedom Song. P

Singing. GP

Before the Throne of Beauty. TS

The Flute. TP (editor's translation from the Arabic)

Beauty. P

Soul of the Dancer. W

An Hour Devoted to Beauty and Love. TS

Life's Human Journey

Your Daily Life Is Your Temple. P
Burying Dead Selves. M
Giving Up a Kingdom. F
Possessions. P
Treasure. SF
The Value of Time. SF
With Senses Continually Made New. JSM. "A Philosopher: On Wonder and Beauty."
Work Is Love. P
Builders of Bridges. W
Renown. SF
Life Is a Procession. SF
Song of Humanity. TS
Singing in the Silence. GP
Modesty. P
Between. SF
Ignorance. SF
When You Meet a Friend. P
Strangers to Life. SF
Life Is a Resolution. MC
Longing. SF
To American Immigrants from the Middle East. YA

Seasons of Life

Changing with the Seasons. BW
No Miracles Beyond the Seasons. JSM. "Melachi of Babylon: An Astronomer."
Youth and Knowledge. SF
Seasons. GP
Autumn and Spring. SF
Time. P
All Your Hours Are Wings. P
Be Dark. SF
Day and Night. GP
Shell-Life. SF
Tides of Breath. P
Shoreless Without a Self. GP
Finding Fault. SF
Every Year I Had Waited for Spring . . . JSM. "Rachel: A Woman Disciple."

Paradoxical Life

Life Comes Walking. GP
Talk. SF
A Tale of Two Tales. W
Confession. SF

Yesterday and Today. TS
Gifts of the Earth. P
Giving and Gaining. P
High and Low. P
Seeking. SF
Freedom. P
Limits. SF
Owl Eyes. P
Voices. SF
Ocean and Foam. P
Blessing Darkness. P
Agreement. SF
Jesus and Pan. JSM. "Sarkis: An Old Greek Shepherd Called the Madman."

The Life of the Soul

Resurrection of Life. JSM. "Nicodemus the Poet: On Fools and Jugglers."
A Fragment. SF
The Greater Sea. M
Truth Is Like the Stars. SR
Have Mercy on Me, My Soul. TS
Trust the Dreams. P

The Greater Self. F
Rising. SF
Children of Space. P
Leave Me, My Blamer. TS
The Forerunner. F
Walk Facing the Sun. P
Soul's Dewdrop. GP
Roots Between. GP
Self Is a Sea. P
The Longing of the Giant Self. P
Angels and Devils. SF
Blessed Mountain. SF
Song of the Soul. TS

About the Author

Dates from the life of Gibran Khalil Gibran, the author's full Arabic name, which due to a registration spelling mistake at his first school in the United States was changed from the usual spelling to "Kahlil."

1883: Born in Bsharri, a village in the north of Lebanon.

1895: Gibran's mother immigrates to Boston with her four children, hoping to flee poverty and unhappiness, while her husband remains in Lebanon, imprisoned for embezzling from the government.

1898: Returns to Lebanon to study Arabic and French at a Maronite-run preparatory school in Beirut. By some accounts, his mother wants to remove him from unsavory artistic influences in Boston.

1902: Returns to Boston. In fifteen months' time, he loses his mother, sister, and half-brother to tuberculosis.

1904: Through photographer Fred Holland Day meets Mary Haskell, a school headmistress, who becomes his patron, muse, editor, and possible lover. Publishes several poems in prose gathered later under the title *A Tear and a Smile*.

1908-10: Funded by Mary, he attends art school in Paris.

1911: Settles in New York where he starts an intimate correspondence with May Ziadeh, a Lebanese intellectual living in Cairo.

1918: *The Madman,* Gibran's first book written in English, is published.

1920: Together with other Arab and Lebanese writers and poets living in the United States, he founds a literary society called *Al Rabita al Qalamiyyah* (The Pen Bond).

1923: *The Prophet* published with immediate success. Begins friendship with Barbara Young who later becomes his new muse and editor.

1928: *Jesus The Son of Man* published.

1931: Dies in a hospital in New York at the age of 48, due to cirrhosis of the liver. As was his wish, his body is transferred in 1932 to Lebanon and is buried in his native town of Bsharri. An old monastery is purchased, which becomes a museum in his memory.

These bare facts belie the complexity and turbulence of Kahlil Gibran's life, both inner and outer. As one of his biographers, Suheil Bushrui, writes:

> The more that has been written about Gibran, the more elusive the man himself has tended to become, as critics, friends, and biographers have built up a variety of unconnected pictures. Gibran himself is partly to blame. He wrote very little about his own life, and in recurrent moments of insecurity and "vagueness," particularly during his first years of recognition, often fabricated or embellished his humble origins and troubled background. This self-perpetuation of his myth—a tendency followed by other literary figures such as Yeats and Swift—was not intellectual dishonesty, but a manifestation of the poetic mind's desire to create its own mythology (Bushrui, 1998).

A good online biography can be found at the website of the Gibran National Committee: *www.gibrankhalilgibran.org*.

As Bushrui notes, the many biographies and biographical studies of Gibran do not agree on many points. They are very much like the different voices presented in Gibran's book *Jesus The Son of Man*, each reporting various facets of a person who embraced both the highs and lows, the lights and shadows of a fully human life.

A selection of the biographies and collections of Gibran's letters is below.

Bushrui, S., and J. Jenkins. (1998). *Kahlil Gibran: Man and Poet*. Oxford: Oneworld.

Bushrui, S., and S. H. al-Kuzbari (eds. and trans.). (1995). *Gibran: Love Letters*. Oxford: Oneworld.

Gibran, J., and K. Gibran. (1974). *Kahlil Gibran: His Life and World*. Boston: New York Graphic Society.

Hilu, V. (1972). *Beloved Prophet: The Love Letters of Kahlil Gibran and Mary Haskell and Her Private Journal*. New York: Alfred Knopf.

Naimy, M. (1950). *Kahlil Gibran: A Biography*. New York: Philosophical Library.

Waterfield, R. (1998). *Prophet: The Life and Times of Kahlil Gibran*. New York: St. Martin's Press.

Young, B. (1945). *This Man from Lebanon: A Study of Kahlil Gibran*. New York: Alfred Knopf.

About the Compiler

Photo by William A. Matheiu

Neil Douglas-Klotz, PhD is a renowned writer in the fields of Middle Eastern spirituality and the translation and interpretation of the ancient Semitic languages of Hebrew, Aramaic, and Arabic. Living in Scotland, he directs the Edinburgh Institute for Advanced Learning an for many years was cochair of the Mysticism Group of the American Academy of Religion.

A frequent speaker and workshop leader, he is the author of several books. His books on the Aramaic spirituality of Jesus include *Prayers of the Cosmos, The Hidden Gospel, Original Meditation: The Aramaic Jesus and the Spirituality of Creation,* and *Blessings of the Cosmos.* His books on a comparative view of "native" Middle Eastern spirituality include *Desert Wisdom: A Nomad's Guide to Life's Big Questions* and *The Tent of Abraham* (with Rabbi Arthur Waskow and Sr. Joan Chittister). His books on Sufi spirituality include *The Sufi Book of Life: 99 Pathways of the Heart for the Modern Dervish* and *A Little Book of Sufi Stories*. His biographical collections of the works of his Sufi teachers include *Sufi Vision and Initiation* (Samuel L. Lewis) and *Illuminating the Shadow* (Moineddin Jablonski). He has also written a mystery novel set in the first century C.E. Holy Land entitled *A Murder at Armageddon*.

For more information about his work, see the website of the Abwoon Network *www.abwoon.org* or his Facebook page *https://www.facebook.com/AuthorNeilDouglasKlotz/*.